AF472410

Valli's Valley

Ex-Nun Reveals All!

Valli - December 1953

Valli's Valley

Ex-Nun Reveals All

by

Valli Louise Dennis Schieltz

EDITED by

Glenn F. Dennis

Foreword by

Rev. Ed Ellis

TigersTime Studios

2015

Valli's Valley: Ex-Nun Reveals All!

First Printing: 2015

ISBN: 978-1-329-12991-7

TigersTime Studios
5225 Banks Haven Ct
Raleigh, NC 27603-8957

www.TigersTimeStudios.com

Ordering Information:

Special discounts are available on quantity purchases by corporations, associations, educators, and others. For details, contact the publisher at the above listed address.

U.S. trade bookstores and wholesalers:

Please contact TigersTime Studios

Phone: (919) 662-1850 or email savage@TigersTimeStudios.com.

Dedication

I would like to thank my loving and supportive husband for standing beside me 100% of the time. I would also like to thank my devoted and loving brother for accepting the challenge of being my brother. He and I would brainstorm ideas back and forth about my book, and he would keep me on the straight and narrow road to completion.

Contents

Dedication vii
Acknowledgments xi
Forward xiii
Preface xv
Introduction xvii
Chapter 1: Alone in the Desert 1
Chapter 2: A Hidden Treasure 7
Chapter 3: Diamonds in the Rough 9
Chapter 4: Baking Mania 11
Chapter 5: Fishing Frenzy 15
Chapter 6: Jesus is the Reason 17
Chapter 7: Penitential Practices 19
Chapter 8: My Prize Possession 25
Chapter 9: Twister 37
Chapter 10: More Mouthwatering Morsels 45
Chapter 11: Thorns into Roses 47
Chapter 12: Let's Pretend 51
Chapter 13: Favoritism 55
Chapter 14: Red Hot Rebuttal 59
Chapter 15: Final Kick in the Pants 61
Epilogue 65
More Photos 67
Addendum 95

Acknowledgments

With a heart filled with gratitude, I would like to thank the following people who not only provided inspiration by example but also were instrumental in crafting proper structure and layout for this book.

Glenn F. Dennis
Father Angelo Caserta
Father James Duelle
Father Martin Fox
Father Tom Bolte
Father Thomas Grilliot
Reverend Ed Ellis

There are numerous nuns and sisters who taught me the right way to go about doing things as well as the wrong way, which tends to disedify. Clothes only show the outward appearance of a person. Some of the religious who I will forever remember are:

Sr. Mary St. Joseph
Sr. Mary Miles
Mother Mary Anthony
Mother Marie Alma
Mother Mary Theresita

Friends and family who lent their loving support and encouragement along the way are my husband, Fred, Matthew Schieltz, Meredith Schieltz, Michaella Schieltz and my two best friends, Betty O'Brien and Carol Popp. Thank you Rev. Ellis for writing the Foreword.

If I left anyone out, it was a mere oversight on my part.

Many thanks. God bless and keep you.

Valli

Foreword

by

Rev. Ed Ellis

"It is my pleasure to write a word of honor and respect for Valli, and the completion of the book which she has written from her heart. Valli and I have shared conversations of courage and spiritual strength. She has gifted me with the insight into the journey of life which has brought her to this place, and gifted me a second time with the invitation to contribute these words. Valli's response of patterning her life to reflect her welcome of God's guidance has been an inspiration for many years. Truly I admire the many ways in which Valli has seen her opportunity to be a servant of God. It takes a humble and obedient spirit to prefer this above all else. May the richness of what she has written bless the reader, and be a source of pride to each of us who have treasured her smile, her gentle spirit, and her loving sense of humor. As I prepare to deliver these words to Valli I anticipate that the prayer time we will share will be yet one more encouragement to the blessing which has been been prepared for each of us. I am reminded of a passage of Scripture which respectfully encouraged Bruce Wilkinson's writing, *The Prayer of Jabez*;

"There was a man named Jabez who was more honorable than any of his brothers. His mother named him Jabez because his birth had been so painful. He was the one who prayed to the God of Israel, 'Oh, that you would bless me and expand my territory. Please be with me in all that I do, and keep me from all trouble and pain.' And God granted him his request." 1 Chronicles 4: 9-10

With great respect,

Rev. Ed Ellis

Hospice of Miami County

March 5, 2015

Preface

I call upon God's Spirit to guide me with His words. I feel that if His Words will inspire the heart of even one person to come and walk a little closer with Jesus, then everything will have been worthwhile. I am reminded of one of my favorite passages in the Holy Bible. This is taken from the 1st Book of Kings Chapter 19: 11 through 13:

Elijah Meets God at Horeb - 11: He said, 'Go out and stand on the mountain before the Lord, for the Lord is about to pass by.' Now there was a great wind, so strong that it was splitting mountains and breaking rocks in pieces before the Lord, but the Lord was not in the wind; and after the wind an earthquake, but the Lord was not in the earthquake; 12: and after the earthquake a fire, but the Lord was not in the fire; and after the fire a sound of sheer silence. 13: When Elijah heard it, he wrapped his face in his mantle and went out and stood at the entrance of the cave. Then there came a voice to him that said, 'What are you doing here, Elijah?'14: He answered, 'I have been very zealous for the Lord, the God of hosts....

It seems that much of the time we look for God in things that are spectacular and that tend to ruffle our feathers. All that the Lord asks of us is that we turn 100% of our lives over to our Heavenly Father.

Now I invite you, the reader, to not seek God in flash floods, avalanches, fires, tsunamis or even the clanging and clashing of thunder. Seek the Lord in the small, gentle breezes of your every day life so that together we may say: 'With zeal I have been zealous for the Lord God of Hosts.'

It really is funny how our Lord works sometimes. When I first received the summons to write about my experience about being a nun, I was still living at home. Every time I would sit at the computer to begin to write, I would experience some distraction or receive a visitor. Or when I would have my aides come to help me, I felt like I had to suddenly act the part of entertainer. So, Jesus saw that something needed to be done so that I would be able to throw 100% of myself into bringing this book to full fruition. He had an ingenious idea.

Do you think Jesus was chuckling to Himself as He thought of the perfect plan so that I would have the best of both worlds? Ah, yes, this was the most ingenious plan the Holy Trinity had since the very beginning of the creation of the world!

I will have to turn back Father Time, all the way back until 1970. I had just gotten word that the reason I had been feeling so crappy is because the blood test I had taken revealed I had a raging case of infectious mononucleosis. I was quarantined in the Carmelite Monastery. I was able to get deep down and personal with Jesus and listen to the prompting of the Holy Spirit.

Today, I am in Genesis Health Care. What an ingenious idea. The Lord directed me here so I could concentrate 100% of my time on prayer, fasting and working on my book without the distractions I experienced at home.

Introduction

1...2...3...Heaven Calling

One of the first questions you may be asking yourself when you first purchased this book is: "How does the Lord call a certain person to enter the religious life?" Just as the heavens contain an infinite array of stars, so everyone's call is distinct. Here's something else to ponder. How does a convert to Catholicism end up becoming a nun? Read on to discover how I was called to the religious life and how a person very close to my heart attempted to thwart the call that Jesus placed deep within its recesses.

Blast from my Past

"It was the best of times, it was the worst of times..." I was born a teeny, little babe, on March 3rd, 1951. I was named Valli Louise Dennis. Could I know of the myriad experiences that would beset me in my lifetime? Was I enlightened by some Celestial Power or was my spirit imbued with only premonitions of what was to befall me? I reflect the quote by the famous author Charles Dickens, who wrote the classic novel, <u>A Tale of Two Cities</u>, "it was the spring of hope, it was the winter of despair; we had everything before us, we had nothing before us…." So it would be for this 7pound 7ounce bouncing baby girl who entered the lives of her father, James Harold Dennis, her mother, Louise Natalie Yanson Dennis, and her brother,

Glenn Forrest Dennis, on the first Saturday of the month at 12:27 P.M. in Tampa, Florida.

As I lay placidly slumbering in my bassinet, it would seem that my restful times of sleep were preparing this innocent baby for what was to happen during the rest of my life. Was my inner psyche linked deep within the bosom of God, her eternal Father? Was the spirit of Darkness even now encircling this spotless infant?

Name Game

As time continues to march on, the name of "Valli" has intrigued a sea of inquisitive people. Therefore, I wish to lay at rest any other wondering minds who may still be searching for the answer as to how I came to be known as "Valli".

When I was still in my mother's womb, Mom had been reading a book about a French movie actress named 'Valli'. Apparently, this was the sole name of this mysterious woman. Hopefully, your curiosity has now been quenched so that I may continue with the meat and potatoes of this ex-nun's tale.

"In The Beginning..."

For starters, I was not a cradle Catholic. In order to bridge the gap between the lay and religious life, I must digress to my travel clock by some fifty-one years to the twelfth year of my unsettled life. As Paul Harvey so succinctly stated, "***...and now for the rest of the story....***"

Topsy-Turvy

Have you ever wondered, as I have, how a person's life can abruptly change course? That is exactly what happened to my brother and me - all within the brief time span of seven months. Our young lives circumstantially went into a tailspin.

I was only twelve years old when my brother and I were summoned by our principal to gather up all of our school books and proceed to hop into the back seat of the pastor's car. Pastor Craig had not even left the school parking lot when he blurted out this brusque remark: "Children, I have something to tell you; your father just died unexpectedly of a massive heart attack." There was no preparation, no softening of the tragedy that was unfolding and certainly no kind of favorable bedside manner...no NOTHING!!! I recall that I let out a halfhearted scream because at the very beginning I felt that our mother met with a bizarre twist of fate. Why did this cross my mind at a time like this? Our father was a bitter, destructive alcoholic who detested me as a queer fluke of nature. However, when Denny was sober it was like reliving Jekyll and Hyde who had two distinct personalities trapped in one, lone body.

After the turmoil of our dad's hastened death at age 43; after friends and neighbors traipsed through the house leaving casseroles and other food items, it was time to get down to brass tacks. Our mom was simply surmising the situation in order to speak to Glenn and me concerning a delicate topic – religion. Perhaps Louise had an enlightenment from the Holy Spirit as to how she would broach her brief broadcast. Mom told Glenn and me that she was not going to hold us to follow any certain religious denomination. She felt that when the time came we would be better equipped to follow Jesus with an arsenal of newly found knowledge at our beck-and-call.

It was not until I was a sophomore at James Island High School that I became an explosive, ticking time-bomb. Corrosive personality uncertainties that were lodged deep within my brain's psyche gushed forth like a raging river on an unruly rampage. Uncertainties spewed out of my body like Old Faithful at Yellowstone National Park. Destructive forces led indelible signs of suicide on my young body. I was hurting so bad mentally that one of my high school friends instructed me to seek a priest's counsel. I was plagued with skepticism as I unwaveringly took baby steps to the Church of the Nativity to meet with Father C. Although his personality was unpleasant, he did not attempt to mince his sage advice.

Inside the Tummy of the Big Bird

This may be the shortest paragraph of Valli's Valley! When I was just a few weeks old, our mom decided that Glenn and I should take a trip to New Jersey to see our grandmother and grandfather. Since mom didn't drive, she decided that we would travel by plane or "the Big Bird" as our father nicknamed airplanes every time he had to travel. You will see a picture of us when we just got off the "Big Bird".

Time Line

March 3, 1951 - 12:27 PM: I, Valli Louise Dennis, was welcomed into this world by James H. Dennis (father), Louise Y. Dennis, (mother), and Glenn F. Dennis (aka Jason Savage), her 22 month old brother, at Tampa Memorial Hospital in western Florida.

Monday, April 23, 1963: Our father, James, dies of a sudden, massive heart attack at age 43.

August, 1963: Our maternal grandfather, Stephan, dies of long bout with pancreatic cancer.

October 23, 1968: Baptism into the Roman Catholic faith. First Confession

October 28, 1968: First Holy Communion

November 22, 1961: Assassination of President John F. Kennedy. Our fraternal grandfather, Morrison, dies of a heart attack.

May 26, 1969: My High School Graduation Day

June 1- August 1, 1969: Preparing to attend nursing school in Missouri. During this time, I made a visit to a Carmelite monastery in Jefferson City, Missouri. I felt I had an inner calling to become a nun there.

August 22, 1969: I decided not to attend nursing school. I entered the Carmelite Monastery and took the name Sister Carmen Marie.

Mid 1971: I made the decision that I had to leave the Carmelite Monastery due to a personality clash between me and the Mother SubPrioress.

January of 1972: I entered a newer branch of the Sisters of Charity in Connecticut under the name Sister Mary Josepha.

May 16, 1980: I left the Sisters of Charity.

January 22, 1981: I met my future husband through mail correspondence.

August 1, 1981: Frederick E. Schieltz and I were married.

Reflections

As I sit here contemplating how Jesus and I are going to attack the Big "C" (surely you guessed CANCER), my mind wanders back to yesteryear, to the time I stood at the turnstile door of the Discalced Carmelite Nuns. These nuns were shrouded in mystery, and I was determined to 'crack the code', so to speak, to see what made these nuns tick! Yet, I wanted to eventually don the habit and hemp sandals that these nuns wore. Are there any juicy tidbits I want to get off my chest? You bet there are, so read on to discover the rest of my story.

Chapter 1: Alone in the Desert

I had not been at Carmel very long before I began to feel overcome with extreme fatigue. Even when I was in line to go and pray in the chapel or to participate in the Mass, it felt like I was being blown-away with an even bigger onslaught. While I knelt down and waited

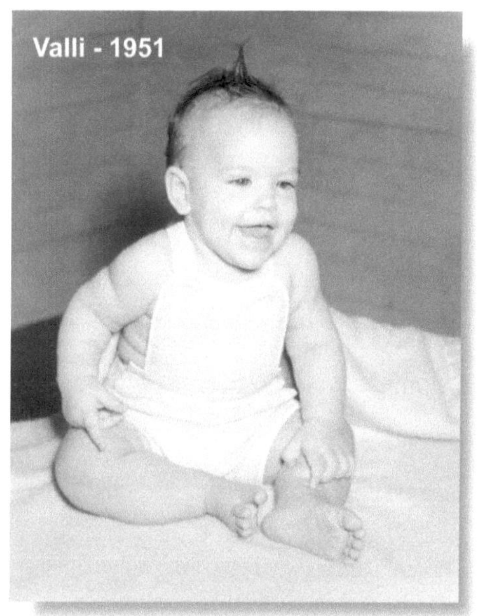
Valli - 1951

to enter the chapel, all of us were given the signal to kiss the floor. This was viewed to be an act of humility in the Eyes of the Lord. For me, Sr. Carmen Marie, this was sheer torture! My head and neck felt like they were on the verge of exploding! I knew I would have to go to the Mother Prioress for help. She immediately called the doctor. He merely felt that I had contracted an infection of some kind and that penicillin would knock this bug right out of me! I had to be given injections, but there was not one nun in the cloister who was qualified to do this.

There was a retired nurse living outside of the cloister who took care of preparing everything for daily Mass who would be perfect for the job. Rose, the nurse, offered to give me the shots. Every day I would see Rose for my daily dose of the cure! Things were not as up to date as they are today. If a shot was to be administered, there would be a plunger and a vial of the prescribed medication. Rose would place the vial of penicillin into the plunger and then administer this medication to me in the arm.

After receiving a few of these miracle injections I was feeling no better, so I went to the Mother Prioress to ascertain just how many times I was going to have to undergo this *torment*. Mother Prioress prophetically stated that I would have to have twenty-one injections. I was growing very weary of visiting Rose for my daily fix.

One day I went to visit Rose, and things were in disarray! Apparently Rose received the vials of penicillin but had no plunger. I could not return to the monastery without acquiring my dosage of penicillin. Rose looked around the room for something that would act as a plunger. Aha! Wandering eyes landed on a pair of scissors that this old nurse felt would adequately do the trick. Rose proceeded to stick the vial into my arm. She then took the scissors and tried pushing the rubber plunger. As I stood frozen in disbelief, I looked on with horror as the scissors proceeded to shatter the glass vial. “Get that thing out

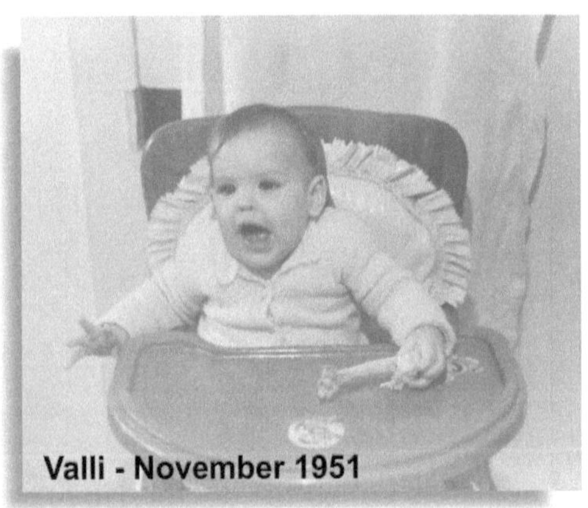
Valli - November 1951

of my arm right NOW!", I screamed. That concluded the fiasco of my visiting Rose for daily injections. I might add that before all was said and done, I had received exactly twenty-one injections! Sheepishly I asked "Our Little Mother" to call the doctor and request that I get a blood test. Why? Read on to discover my next adventure that took place behind enclosed walls.

Valli and Glenn - 1953

The doctor delivered the distressing diagnosis over the telephone. I had contracted infectious mononucleosis from using a glass that my brother had used earlier when we both happened to be home at the same time. Wow! This was just my LUCK! My future was in the hands of 'Our Little Mother'! The verdict was in, and now I had to listen like an obedient little child as the sentence was pronounced. I was to be quarantined until the disease ran its course. The only thing I could participate in with the other nuns was the Holy Mass. I had to eat alone, wash my dishes in Clorox, drink lots of juice and rest, since mono makes a person feel totally zapped of energy.

That straw mattress and pillow now looked awfully enticing!

During this time I was alone in the "desert" I grew much closer to Jesus, especially the Crucified Christ, the Suffering Messiah. I can recall that even in my childhood I would pretend to be crucified just like Our Lord. I would pretend to be nailed to the clothes pole just

Glenn, Chess, and Valli - June 1953

like Jesus was nailed to the Cross when He reached Calvary. I would pattern my whole life after the Crucified Christ. However, it would be many years later that my role on this earth would be clearly defined. Suffice it for now to leave Sr. Carmen Marie alone in the desert" to be strengthened not only by the Body and Blood of Christ but by all the time that was spent alone with her Lover. It was during these months of quarantine that Jesus would imbue this sister with the strength to overcome the onslaughts of the devil. However, I would have to be swallowed up by this foreboding valley and experience its distressing depths before I could climb to the mountain top to bask in the Glory of the Blessed Trinity! This would happen many times during my life because the closer one comes to Jesus, the more one is tried in the crucible of suffering.

Valli, Louise, and Glenn - 1954

I was to be kept in "this desert place" for three long months with only Jesus for my constant Companion. Who else would I need? I was able to eat, drink, breathe and meditate Jesus without having any distractions. This was indeed a great grace! However, many times I was so tired that all I could do was to plop down on my mattress of straw and fall promptly to sleep. For those who have been afflicted with infectious mononucleosis, this is one characteristic everyone experiences – periods of extreme malaise that nothing can cure but rest.

Valli and Glenn - Shore Acres, NJ
June 1956

There was yet another 'cure' that was thrust upon me and that was to drink as much juice as I could tolerate, and that amounted to about a gallon a day. This would be sure to cleanse my system of all impurities!

The day finally came when my blood-work came back CLEAN! This was when I could finally break free of my quarantine. However, I had to perform one more task before I would be allowed to join the other nuns. I had to empty the straw from my mattress and pillow and stuff all new straw into the pillow case and mattress casing. Now I was FREE!

Chapter 2: A Hidden Treasure

Here was another adventure in the life of Sr. Carmen Marie that may kindle a fire within the hearts of all animal lovers. I remember that I was out digging in the garden when, all of a sudden, I pulled up some of the earth on my shovel, and there I was staring down at four prairie dogs that had just been born.

Each of them had a high-pitched wail. What in the world should I do? I hurriedly whisked them off to Mother SubPrioress in the hopes that she could shed some light on the subject. She coldly looked down at the tiny pups and barked, “Kill them!” I immediately shook my head 'No' and headed off in search of 'Our Little Mother'. When I managed to find her, I was so distraught that I nearly cried when I told Her Prioress what I was instructed to do with these helpless, little critters. She gently took them from me. I could not look back. I never learned the destiny of the adorable baby prairie dogs, and I think that God wanted it that way. Unlike Lot's wife who was tempted to look back to view the fate of Sodom and Gomorrah, I set my face like flint toward the Son!

Valli and Fred together at St. Boniface Church, Piqua, on July 23, 2005, for their son's wedding.

Chapter 3: Diamonds in the Rough

Here is another very amusing animal tale that may interest corn crop growers. It seemed that the nuns' corn crop was slowly doing a disappearing act. Who or what could be stripping the cornstalks bare? This was getting to be rather unnerving! One day a light bulb went off in one of the cooking nun's mind. She was going to park herself in a strategic location and wait up all night if she had to in order to blow the whistle on this sneaky varmint! Here is what I

Valli, James, and Glenn - 1956

discovered. You know what was at the bottom, or I should say at the top, of this cornstalk caper? RATS!! It was quite ingenious of these ugly, gray rodents. Each rat supported another on its back until it was able to reach the highest edible ear of corn. It was then that this delectable delicacy was stripped bare of its kernels. This was done repeatedly until every ear on the cornstalk was chewed clean. These rats really had their system down pat! Imagine how it looked to see half of the corn crop stripped! Since I had exposed these rats for what they were, you can imagine that the nuns never had another corn crop succumb to the aching bellies of these ravenous rats! At last, another mystery solved behind the closed, cloistered Carmelite enclosure.

Glenn and Valli - December 1957

Chapter 4: Baking Mania

A source of primary income for this motley-minded group of austere Carmelites was to provide surrounding cities and towns with altar breads that were to be used at Masses in the Catholic churches. I must say that I took to this task like an old pro! I loved being able to bake the bread that would become the Sacred Body of Jesus Christ and would touch the hearts of so many people.

Louise, Copper, and Valli - 1/1/1957

I realized that I not only had to be quick-minded but sure-footed as I learned to race around these three ovens like the Mad Hatter himself! I really had no time to daydream on the job. I simply reacted to the sights and sounds of the cold batter on the sizzling ovens spewing out the molten material on all four sides of each of these roasting receptacles! With sharp-edged scraper in hand, I briskly broke into a determined dash around the room deftly scraping the seething, sizzling batter that was oozing out around all four sides of each oven. I was to keep up this grueling pace until I was relieved some two terribly tiring hours later. By this time, some salty sweat lazily lumbered down my weary, worn countenance and continued to drench the fibers of my brown Carmelite habit.

When I was allowed to leave the premises of the baking room, it was customary for me to retreat to the Novitiate and slip into my cell (room), grab a clean, crisp habit and showering supplies and wend my way to the lavatory where I would relax under the refreshing beads of water that rained down all over my bare body. As soon as I was sufficiently squeaky clean, I would quickly step out of the shower, towel off and don my dry habit. Then I would hurriedly glance at the clock to see if I would have enough time to begin my next "mission for Jesus" or if He was whispering to me to hasten to the Chapel for Vespers (afternoon prayer). I used to love to hear Sister Mary L. chant the Gregorian Chant with her clear, sweet, operatic voice. At that time, I had a resonating voice that was right on pitch, and I too was able to learn some of the Gregorian Chant of the Divine Office.

Glenn and Valli - 1957

When all of us nuns had finished chanting Vespers, we then said the rosary and afterward had a half hour of meditation. If one's knees were in good condition, then the correct posture for both the recitation of the rosary and meditation was in a kneeling position. I usually grew weary so I sat back on my lower legs to give my knees a much-needed break!

Valli - September 1958

Valli with Michaella - on 7/23/2005
at Matthew's wedding reception.

Chapter 5: Fishing Frenzy

There is one bad memory that I had when I was in the monastery (only 1?!!). This time all of us were gathered in the dining area which was known as the Refectory. We all took turns being servers. This one particular time we were being served fish. I looked at my plate rather dubiously and then took a bite. Low and behold I got a catch! What should have lodged in the roof of my mouth was the

Valli, Louise, and Glenn - May 1958

biggest fish bone I have ever felt! I began to appraise the situation to see what to do next. Should I go to the center of the Refectory and motion to Our Mother to allow me to leave so I could retrieve this obtrusive fish bone, or should I just matter-of-factly sit at my place pretending that everything was A-OK? I decided to do the latter, but I still had to get this fish bone out from the poor, punctured roof of my mouth. Well, I just did what came naturally! I opened my mouth wide, took my thumb and first finger, thrust them into my mouth and securely locked them around this unwelcome guest. I had to jiggle the bone back and forth until the roof of my mouth decided to set the fish bone free! Do you think anyone had a clue of what just went on? If any of the nuns suspected anything, no one mentioned it.

Valli - May 1959

Chapter 6: Jesus is the Reason

The most festive and decorative feast in this Carmelite monastery in Missouri was the feast of Christmas when Jesus came down to earth and humbled Himself becoming man. This would begin His thirty-three year journey culminating in His death on the Cross and the pouring out of His Most Precious Blood for the forgiveness of our sins. Do not take this lightly! Jesus loves YOU so MUCH that if He had to do it all over again He would NOT hesitate. Yet, first Jesus had to come down as a tender, tiny baby, completely dependent upon Mary and Joseph for EVERYTHING!

Valli and Glenn - Christmas 1959

The spirit in the monastery was of heightened anticipation of the coming of the Messiah. Every sister was to make a one-day retreat as she awaited the long-heralded birth of Jesus. This was the time in which she would divest her soul of every frivolous element, sweep it clean of even the most minute venial (easily excused) sin so as to make her soul a spotless 'manger' that will cradle the newborn Baby Jesus.

Louise and Valli - Florida 1959

This was not only a time for intense introspection, but the monastery needed to have an additional spring cleaning because the bishop usually paid his little flock a visit during the Christmas season. I would usually be the one to tackle the huge buffer to give the monastic floor a highly polished sheen. Other nuns would man their stations at the tall, slender windows to make them shine like a shimmering sea of glass. Last but not least, a group of nuns would get on board the cleaning crew armed with mops and cloths to wipe down the monastic walls to send all the cobwebs into everlasting obliteration. Even though we nuns could barely contain our smug smiles of satisfaction, our tedious toil was well worth the effort for the bishop gracing us with his presence.

Chapter 7: Penitential Practices

Do not be fooled! It was not merely prayer or fasting or simply fun and games either. There was a seriousness about each nun's demeanor and countenance which indicated that by their profession of the solemn vows of poverty, chastity and obedience that each nun definitely was into this austere way of life for the LONG haul.

There were many acts of penance that even the youngest of the nuns could do, and that would have been me. Any lay person can perform a variety of penitential acts if they make the proper intention. Could it really have taken me over forty years to master this concept. Many times I will simply offer my acts of Love to Jesus to be applied where they are most needed.

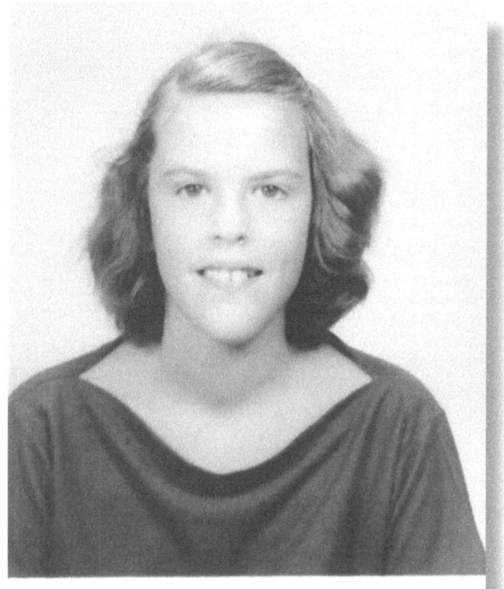

There are a few acts of penance that still remain embedded in my memory to this day. Lent was a huge penitential season in the Discalced Carmelite Monastery. The Black Fast was one of the hardest things for me to get used to. According to the Catholic Encyclopedia, “This form of fasting, the most rigorous in the history of church legislation, was marked by austerity regarding the quantity and quality of food permitted on fasting...” Usually that meant no meat during the whole Lenten season of forty days. Then on Good Friday, the fast tightened its grip on each nun because only bread and water was eaten.

Fasting was not the only form of penance. There was one act of Love that I put in my spiritual bouquet; that was to kneel by the door leading to the Refectory or dining hall and kiss the foot of each nun as she filed passed. There were a couple of more penitential acts that were carried out in the Refectory - take a meal while sitting on the floor and wear a crown of thorns while carrying a cross.

Valli and Glenn - April 2, 1961

There was one act of penance that we performed in common with lights out in the chapel. This discipline made use of a short whip that had several strands. We nuns would then beat ourselves around our hips. If you wanted to inflict more pain, you just put a bit more gusto into hitting the target area. This was meant to signify Jesus as He was scourged at the pillar.

The last penitential rite consisted of wearing chains on different parts of one's body – arms, legs and waist. The chain itself, made in all sorts of sizes, consisted of sharp-edged barbs of wire backed by pieces of brown cloth and strings that could be tightened at the nun's discretion. The cloth covered the chain so no one would have an inkling of what the nun was offering up to her Bridegroom.

Friend, Valli, and Glenn
Folly Beach - 1961

When it came time to profess my temporary vows, which were renewed each year for five successive years, I had to make a gigantic, life altering decision. Every nun cast either a white or black ball (marble) for a yay or nay. There could be **no** black ball! Unfortunately, the second highest ranking official was Mother Sub-prioress. To my dismay, she and I had a severe personality clash. I knew that this unrelenting nun would just as soon thrust a knife in my back than to allow me to stay at my beloved Carmel. (I do want to take the opportunity to forgive the Mother Sub-prioress for all the wrong she did to me and to ask forgiveness if I did anything against her.) Therefore, I began to do some heavy soul searching in order to know God's Divine will.

I wonder even now what would have happened if I would have chosen to wait out the eye of the storm? I had enough pride left

Piano Recital - May 21, 1962

that I chose to leave Carmel and not be booted out into the raucous riptide of a very undisturbed sea of sisters. As I mentioned previously, the vote had to be unanimous and not just a majority of white or black balls. (Photo below was taken at Hanahan Hall)

I decided that I did have enough pride to quit the cloister under my own volition and not just be tossed out. Yet, even to this day, January 14th, 2015, a delicate part of my heart still remains within my beloved Carmelite cloister as I often ponder what may have been. The Lord knows even now how my heart silently aches to be Sister Carmen Marie again. However, I am sure if this would have been God's Holy Will for me, then undoubtedly, He would have made a way for me to remain hidden behind these monastic walls.

Thus ends the first episode as a Carmelite nun. I still had a lot to learn about discerning exactly what Jesus had in store for the rest of my life. I had to place ALL of my trust in the Hands of Jesus. It seems like the back of my life's tapestry was a plethora of jumbled knots. When I reach the summit of God's mountain, then will I behold the spectacular picture Jesus had been painting all along. As I have so succinctly stated, God's timing is perfect! My Lord would again take

Valli and Glenn - 1962

up His pruning shears and trim away all unsightly branches.

Next, I will take you into the majority of my life as a Sister of Charity of Our Lady of the Roman Catholic Church. This is where some things become rather dicey.

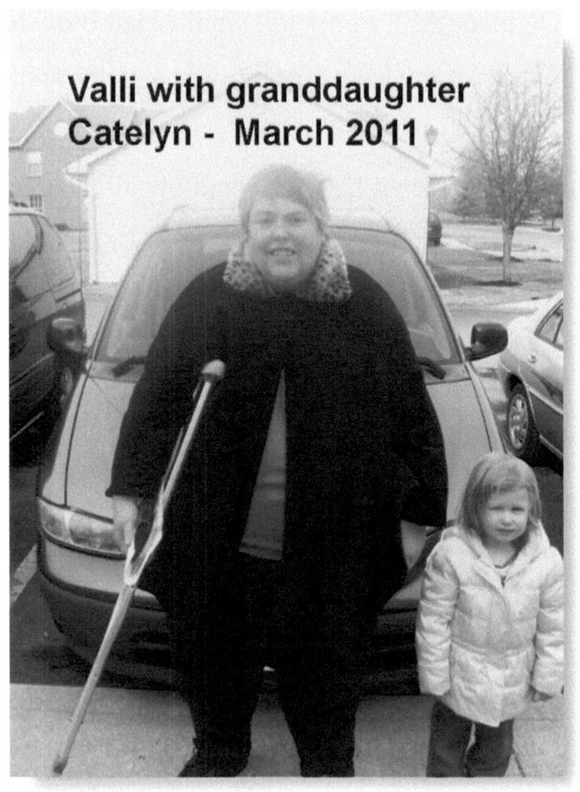
Valli with granddaughter Catelyn - March 2011

Chapter 8: My Prize Possession

I made a few side trips to a city near Madison, Wisconsin. A small contingent of sisters was looking to merge with a more traditional order of Sisters who only revised their outlandish headgear. That is what I was in search of, and that is finally what I found. If only I would have consulted the Holy Spirit from the get-go! Live and learn.

The Cistercian order was much too strict for poor little ole' me, and the climate was too bitterly cold. These sisters must have been made of steel. We worked in the barn as well as baked altar breads. However, it was "Rise and Shine" at 3 A.M. I even had to drink a cup of STRONG, COLD coffee to get through our Morning Prayers. But as soon as I sat down, I was out like a light faster than than you can snuff out a smoldering candlewick! Then, what do you know? Heave ho, lights had to be out by 7 P.M. This was their daily routine. It wasn't for me. This, my friend, was the round about way I ended up in Beemer, Connecticut.

Piano Recital - 1963

This was God's plan for my life all along. It was enough that I be a yielded vessel in the Potter's Hands. It would do me no good to kick against the goad. God's timing is PERFECT! Being a beginner (Postulant) with this newly formed religious order to becoming a Novice (sister in training) along this provocative pathway to temporary vows was exciting.

My disappointment at having to leave my beloved Carmelite monastery turned into spontaneous joy at the prospect of entering a

Copper, Christine (Grandmother), Smokey, Valli, Glenn, and King

traditional order where each sister wore a full length habit was of unspeakable bliss for me. Recall me saying, "When God abruptly slams a door, He invariably opens a window." During this time, boundless love flooded into the secret recesses of my heart as I was giddy with glee at the thought of donning the traditional garb of a

Sister of Charity of Our Lady of the Roman Catholic Church.

There was a copious amount of snow bombarding the windshield as I disembarked the airplane during the winter of 1973. Was the inclement weather a premonition of what was in store for me as I attempted a visualization of the painstaking passageway I would have to suffer for love of the Lord? Could the glistening snowflakes that

Valli's birthday party - March 3, 1963. L/R - Ashley, Glenn, Valli, Marsha, and Terri

greeted me secretly as I clamored into the car an indication that everything was going to be smooth sailing from here on out? Think again, as the rocky road was sure to become bumpier as I set foot into the Mother House of this "charitable" congregation of the Sisters of Charity! Attempting to compare my beloved Carmel to this relatively new order of sisters was like comparing sweet, succulent peaches to sharp, sour lemons. There was simply NO comparison! I had to start all over again as Sister M. Josepha. I took a new name with a new congregation with a brand spanking new set of rules. Just one aspect of religious life remained the same – the permission line! I, along with a majority of sisters, detested standing in line asking for some basic necessities of life such as a toothbrush, tooth paste, bath soap and even begging for permission to retire early due to an illness. I do not know what was going through each sister's mind. I had to wait for at least thirty minutes to reach the superior.

Graduation - May 1969

Such a ritual was extremely humiliating to me. The bush could not grow if some of the superfluous branches were not sheared away first. Only then could the Lord stir the embers of my chilly heart making it suitable for the salvation of souls. This quotation from John 6: 39-40 is a suitable explanation.

"39: And this is the will of him who sent me, that I shall lose none of all that he has given me, but raise them up at the last day. 40: For my Father's will is that everyone who looks to the Son and believes in him shall have eternal life, and I will raise him up at the last day."

Jesus hung on the sweet wood of the cross for what seemed like an eternity. The only aspect of this fragrant tree were the nails which pierced His Hands and Feet. The chief cause of His death was an agonizing asphyxiation. For a brief span of time, these are some of the

Novitiate Entrance

final words uttered from Our Savior's mouth: "*Father, forgive them for they know not what they do*" - and to John, the apostle, Jesus uttered, "*Son, behold thy mother*" - and with a distinct finality as He was sinking down on the nail in His Feet Jesus cried out in a loud voice, "*It is finished*", and Our Lord yielded His Spirit to His Father and died.

I do want to reiterate once more that each time I begin to settle down into my writing mode, I fervently beseech the Holy Spirit to infuse my brain with only His Words. I also ask my Jesus for enlightenment as to what He thinks should be incorporated in this book. Now, take my hand as we traverse through my memories in order to jot them down on paper.

One of the most beautiful flowers growing on Earth today is the rose, with its vast array of vibrant hues. One thing that all these roses have in common is that in order to reach the summit to behold these

Glenn, King, and Valli
Christmas 1972

sweet smelling fragrances, one is surely to be attacked by at least one of the thorny projections protruding from the base of the rose and meandering all the way up to the top, ending with a most picturesque scene of roses ready to be plucked by a fervent flock of sisters. They all wanted to lay claim to several of these delicate beauties in order to decorate the most unadorned spot in Chapel.

I would have my own thoughts frolicking around in my mind about the roses and thorns. I viewed the thorny rose bushes as a means of spiritual growth. I was trained early on in my life as a Sister of Charity of Our Lady of the Roman Catholic Church to offer up each cross in my life for the poorest soul in need of salvation.

Valli and Louise - 1973

Amazingly, Jesus already knows where the graces from my sacrifices should be applied. I think the Lord wanted me to be humble enough to ask Him to apply my spiritual bouquet to the most neglected soul here on earth as well as in purgatory. That brings on a debate of a very heated subject in the Catholic Church today.

Is there a certain place in the Bible which explains the existence of Purgatory? The following quotation is taken directly from The Catechism of the Catholic Church: “All who die in God’s grace, but still imperfectly purified, are indeed assured of their eternal salvation; but after death they undergo purification, so as to achieve the holiness necessary to enter the joy of heaven (1030).

Although the traditional Catholic Church endorses the concept of Purgatory, my interpretation of such a place takes on quite a colorful distinction. I know that some of the Saints who now behold the Beatific Vision pretty much seal the deal on what all good Catholics should believe about those who suffer the pains of Purgatory. This bitter suffering, unlike the pangs of hell, will not last for an eternity. These souls know with deep certainty that their suffering will come to an end. On the other hand, those ugly souls who were condemned to hell will be lost within the agonizing torture of NEVER being able to see God. These castaways have only themselves to blame for their

Valli in front of Trapier Dr. pond - 1973

fate. As I would often relate to my students, "You are writing your own ticket as to where you shall go when you leave your bodily dwelling. The decision was yours all along. At the end, when you stand in front of our merciful God, He is simply going to stamp your ticket *Heaven* or *Hell*. Along life's journey, you have been wracking up points, and God is going to stamp your ticket for your final destination. Therefore, do NOT blame God if you are thrown into everlasting darkness where there will be wailing and gnashing of

teeth. The main suffering in hell is not the fire and brimstone but the reality of never being able to see God or to feel His presence.

I believe the concept of Purgatory can take on different forms. I believe that there are earthly souls who are allowed to be purged of their sins and imperfections so that at the time of their death they may go straight to Heaven with NO stop overs!

It is well worth making note of how one of my Charismatic

Catholic friends looked at the whole view of Purgatory. I can still see Robert Betters with his eyes riveted on Jesus Crucified giving us his rendition of Purgatory. I can look at the copious tears running down his cheeks as Robert bellowed in a crystal clear voice, “Fix your eyes on Jesus crucified on the cross with His Precious Blood running down His swollen and bruised Face. Blood was flowing down his Hands and Feet and is being spilled like the ebb and flow of the ocean tides.”

Valli - 1975

When Jesus finally uttered, “It is finished,” he finally gave up His Spirit to the Father. One of the Roman soldiers, seeing that Jesus was already dead, thrust his lance deep into the side of Jesus and out gushed the very last of His Precious Blood mingled with water. Blood flowed down Jesus' Body and splattered on the parched earth. He spilled every last drop of His Precious Blood to redeem YOU from every sin. If you were the only one on this planet, Jesus would do this all over again because of His tremendous love he has for you!

When it is your turn to leave this earth and stand before your Redeemer, do you really think that Jesus will tell you that you must go to Purgatory and suffer some MORE??? Jesus paid the price ONCE and for ALL. What makes you doubt the power in the Blood of Christ? So, dear friends, is Purgatory a rule given by God, our Merciful and Loving Father, or is it simply a man-made rule? I rest my case." It may have taken me almost fifty years to come to the same conclusion that Robert Betters knew in his heart all along. I am at complete peace knowing that I am going straight up to meet my Jesus.

Tae Kwon Do - October 1995

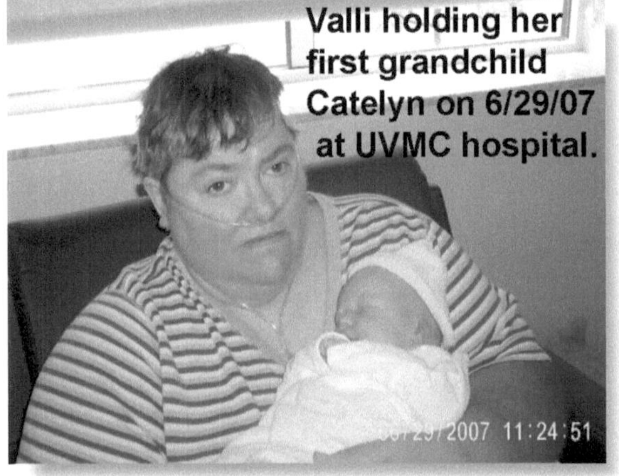

Valli holding her first grandchild Catelyn on 6/29/07 at UVMC hospital.

Chapter 9: Twister

This chapter is a play on words. Hopefully, this is a book that you just cannot bear to put down, so keep reading and see if you can pick out the irony of this chapter.

When I became a postulant with the traditional order of Sisters of Charity (for short), I had to begin the learning process all over again. Only three sisters made up The Novitiate at the time I made my grand entrance into this young order. Since I had a great devotion to St. Joseph, it was only right that I would take on at least a form of 'Joseph'. Since this order already had one Sister Mary Joseph, I would forever be known as Sister M. Josepha. Let's dig deeper to find out if this, my final stay, was going to yield peaches and cream or if some wild, sour grapes made their way into my life.

Convent - 1975

The very first ominous, yet perplexing, cloud that was about to envelope me was so sinister that I felt like I was being covered in a black shroud. Here are the events that preceded the sickening feeling -

like a lead balloon in the pit of my stomach.

As soon as I became a beginner, I was summoned by the Mother General and Mother Foundress because they knew I had a gift for doing amazing embroidery work. I was given the assignment to embroider the picture of Our Lady of Perpetual Help on the front of the chasuble that was to be worn by the priest while he officiated at the Mass. There was no doubt in my mind that I could do it, but I had no idea that I was going to be put on such a stringent schedule.

Baltic, CT - 1975 - Temporary Vows

I had to go over to the school in order to enlarge the picture. I was still there, when all of a sudden Sr. Merci came running over to say I had a long distance telephone call. Before her words even penetrated my heart, I was out of the building like flash. Right away my mind thought that my grandmother did not make it through her surgery. I began to speed up, never once realizing that I had a steep hill to navigate. I was just like a car trying to negotiate the terrain that lay ahead of me. I really wasn't thinking of applying any *brakes*, then something threw me a curve! As I was charging down that hill like a bull in a china shop, my left knee twisted. I felt the cartilage snap like a rubber-band! A dreaded feeling sunk like a two ton concrete block in the bottom of my stomach. Was this to end the once hopeful religious life that I truly felt that Jesus was calling me to? In retrospect, it would have been better to simply say, "Father Knows Best" and submit my will entirely to the Father in Heaven. However, I was so taken up with the newness of this pristine order that I did not even dare to think that the nuns who composed the Sisters of Charity would dare have any faults.

I really felt uptight about approaching Mother Mary Dominic

Val and Danke at Trapier Dr. - 1977

about the accident I had while racing back to the Mother House in order to take that fateful call. It turned out that my grandmother, Pal (nickname for Christine), underwent the surgery like a trooper. This

Novice Mistress, who was given the daunting task of training us greenhorns into model Sisters of Charity, had a gentle and most patient spirit. Not only that, she also had the patience of Job! She saw to it that I got an appointment to see a doctor right way.

After all tests were taken, I had to return to the doctor to get the results. Realistically, the only choice I had was to have surgery. Listening to Dr. Egerton explain it, the surgery seemed rather straightforward. He said that I would have an incision approximately an inch long and would be in and out of the hospital in no time. The doctor also informed me that I would have very little blood loss. Lies, lies, and more lies!!!

Fred and Valli Christmas 1982

After waking up from surgery, I found the incision was every bit of three to four inches long, and I did have quite a bit of blood loss. One thing I was not prepared for was the reality that I had to learn to walk all over again.

There was an unexpected complication that occurred after the torn cartilage was removed that left me totally drained both physically and emotionally. When my temperature spiked at 103 degrees F, I suddenly became frozen with fear! Hastening to find a scrap of paper to write on, I managed to scribble this note to the physician who operated on me. “This is to inform you that this leg is to stay ON my body – NO amputation!”. Despite everything else that went wrong during this 'simple' surgery, I contracted a staph infection and had to be quarantined. When I went back to the convent, I had to undergo some grueling physical therapy to get my knee back into top condition. Every night before going to bed, Mother Anton would have me lay on my stomach. She would grab my foot and bend it back towards my head. OUCH!!

The initial surgery was performed in 1974. Two more operations were performed consecutively by the same Dr. Egerton in 1975 and 1976 to fix the botched up job he did originally. Every time I would step into the permission line at the Mother house, Mother Mary Grimes would just glare at me and shout, “When are you going to STOP all of this nonsense?!! Mother thought that every sister should be the same as she. She would like to see her tight knit band of sisters suffer in silence. Why couldn't everyone be just like her – grin and bear it – and lash out at the poor sister who was next in line with some physical ailment. I quickly found out the if you had a weak constitution, then this order

Fred and Valli - Christmas 1982

was not a suitable place to mend your wounds.

In August of 1977, all of the sisters, young and old, eagerly waited to see what mission house they would be assigned to and who would make up the motley crew for the coming year. This band of the Sisters of Charity had two main functions. Some would be care for the sick and infirmed sisters as they entered their twilight years. Other sisters would enter the teaching force. One thing I never wanted to do was teach school! Well, I supposed that our Loving Father had other plans for me. If He was to prune away all the dry kindling wood that was impeding the growth of the healthy branches, then He was going to have to give me an assignment that was not to my liking.

Christmas Louise and Valli - 1982 Piqua, Ohio

Oh, I could see that wily snake was jumping for joy at the prospect that I would be a full time school teacher. I was told by Mother Anton that I would not just be observing the teacher in the 4th grade, but I was to be teaching that 4th grade. I was given this assignment just two days before school started! My classroom was not even ready!!. You should have seen the camaraderie of fellow teaching sisters who helped me get my classroom into tiptop shape. I will be forever grateful for each and every sister who sacrificed some of their time to help me.

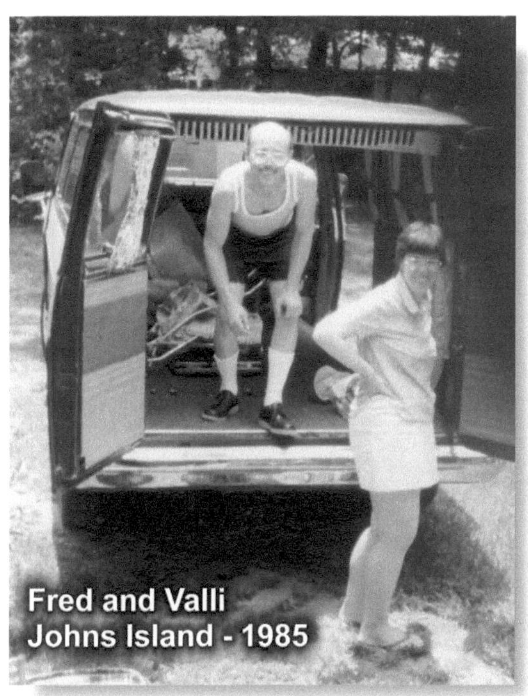
Fred and Valli
Johns Island - 1985

Since I had NO experience as a teacher and had NO college degree, the principal of the school was mildly apprehensive as to how I was going to pull this off. Sister Patrice wanted to come to observe me in action, and I gave her the green light to come on in! After watching me in action, this tiny, energetic, ball of fire called me out into the hallway and lowered the boom. “Sister Josepha, you don't need anyone to observe you. Why, you're a born NATURAL!!”

I could just imagine how that cunning snake in the grass, the devil himself, had to retreat in defeat. Of course, he would always be looking over my shoulder seeking several strategies that would win me over to Lucifer's legions.

Valli, Krysten, Fred, Meredith, and Danke - 1985 -Johns Island

Chapter 10: More Mouthwatering Morsels

Am I simply saving the best for last? You didn't think I was going to string you along all this time and not even mention some of the utterly disgusting things that went on behind locked doors. I just want to reiterate that everything I am writing in this book is the truth. Had I never experienced such politics being played in the different mission houses (all in the United States), I would have shaken my head in disbelief!

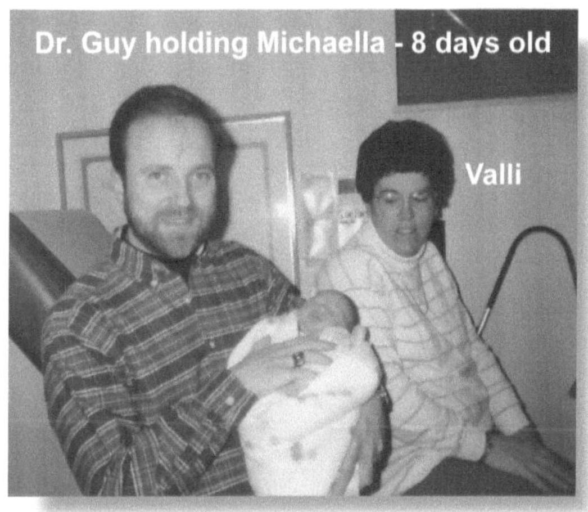

If you happened to be on the good side of some of the top ranking sisters of this newly formed order, then you had it made - that is, you were on easy street. I, on the other hand, was considered the black sheep of the flock. It seems that I was bombarded from all sides. Mr. Devil was going to try his hardest to trip me up and sink me in his quicksand. That would send me rushing into the towering inferno of hell. Not so fast you filthy, fallen angel!! God is my Strength and my Shield against any attack the devil and his cohorts would brandish. Take your best shot, you devilish fiends from the depths of hell. God has my back, so you will always lose!

Valli standing with her son,Matthew, at a school assembly - April 2000.

Chapter 11: Thorns into Roses

I want to fast forward to the present for just a few moments to explain how God can change a disaster into a blessing in disguise. On February 2, 2015, I had an appointment to see Dr. Fuentes. It was time to change my trach tube for a new one. It is a long story as to how I ended up with a tracheostomy.

Valli, Louise, Matthew, Krysten, and Meredith
April 1987

On January 7, 2012, I was in surgery getting my left foot operated on AGAIN. All of a sudden there was trouble in the Operating Room. My left vocal cord was already paralyzed due to a mistake that was made during a previous surgery. Now my right vocal cord was on the verge of collapse. I was literally dying on the table. A split second decision had to be made.

Someone left the O.R. to call in a specialist. He would be able make an immediate decision. Dr. Fuentes lived approximately thirty minutes away from the hospital. He later explained that he had to tell the attendants what to do to keep me alive until he got to the hospital. I remember a nurse was bending over me saying that I did not have to do this if I did not want to.

Valli and Louise
Christmas - Piqua
1997

Seeing that she was very vague about everything, I told the nurse, “let's get it done”. The next thing I knew I woke up in the Intensive Care Unit with my hands strapped to the bed. I was on a ventilator and could not speak. Sometime later, Dr. Fuentes explained that if I had refused to get the trach, I would have died of asphyxiation. Now for the “rest of the story”.

As I previously stated, I had an appointment on the 2nd of February to see Dr. Fuentes in order to change my trach. So I had to make sure to take a new tracheotomy kit with me. To tell the truth, I was not feeling all that well, but I kept this secret to myself for the time being. Guess what? I had NO trach kit to take with me. There was one, but it was not the right size. I ended up having to reschedule the appointment. I am sure God diverted a disaster. I was feeling terribly nauseated. I then had a vision of me in the office waiting for Dr. Fuentes to enter. It was an eerie feeling. When the trach was being changed, I began vomiting. Some of this aspirated into my lungs, and I ended up being rushed to the hospital. Do you not see how God took a negative situation and turned it to a blessing in disguise? All I have to say is, "Thank you, Jesus"!

Valli's children in 1999. From left to right, top to bottom. Krysten, Jenna, Meredith, Matthew, and Michaella

Valli with son, Matthew, in front of the family's home - Spring '04

Chapter 12: Let's Pretend

Let's play a game where audience participation is required. If you are to reap the benefits of this fifth chapter, then you will surely want to throw yourself into the thick of things. Without further adieu, let us jump right in.

Valli and Kitten - 2012

Sr. Josepha was finally transferred to a sleepy, Irish town in Mardock, Connecticut. It would be another year of teaching at the junior high level. The principal of the school was Mother Marie Arton. She may have been small in stature, but she was 100% spitfire. It seemed like this job was right up her alley. I can think of many episodes I would like to include in this chapter, but I will limit the instances to only a few that happened to me while I was teaching.

The arrangement this school used when changing classes was quite unique. Instead of the students going to a different classroom when the bell rang, the teachers would gather up their books and whisk their way to their next room full of smiling students. When the second alarm sounded, it was the signal for teaching to commence.

Since I was already at my destination, I could see that Father

Gordon was just finishing up, or so I thought. The next logical move was to open the door. WRONG!! Father Gordon felt absolutely NO remorse in scowling at me and giving me a stern warning NEVER to do that again. Naturally, I apologized and felt everything was fine. I proceeded to put my books on my desk. I gave instructions to my students to take out their supplies. I wanted to make sure I had ample time to administer my spelling test.

Valli with kitten - '05

All of a sudden it was like a tornado had pushed the classroom door open. It was Mother Anton. Watch out for falling debris!! If you were Mother Anton, how would you have handled this situation?

Option 1: Would Mother Anton call me out into the hallway and proceed to yell at me so that every teacher and student could hear loud and clear what was being said? That would be like the whole school having a front row seat near an intercom! Option 2: Would this little fireball call me to her office and tell me in no uncertain terms that I was NEVER to do that to Father Gordon again? Option 3: This is how the cannonball handled this poor little sister. There I stood, facing my thirty students, preparing to give my spelling test. Mother Anton was screaming in my face, but I had to pretend that nothing was happening.

Valli and her growing family in September '88.

Was this the way a true professional would have handled this problem? I don't think so!!! I now take this opportunity to forgive Mother Anton for all the anguish she caused me. To forget will be a lot more difficult. The following quotation fits this situation to a tee; "To err is human; to forgive is divine."

How about those roads? Whoever planned Mardock's roadway system had to have been a bit tipsy and probably the thought never occurred to him, or her, to ask for advice from his colleagues. What a jumbled up jigsaw puzzle this city's road system turned out to be. I was not a seasoned driver, and my sense of direction, especially in a new town, was not especially well developed. I certainly remember more than one instance when I would tussle with the superior of the house about how my sense of direction was all bottled up inside my big toe!!

Valli with daughter Jenna (3.5 weeks old) - August '89

What kind and charitable words left Mother Anton's gravely, gruff lips. There were lots of little skirmishes here and there over my getting lost all the time when I did the driving. All I had to do was to keep my mouth shut. Jesus was attempting to prune back the ugly branches of pride in order for new foliage to have a chance to grow.

Chapter 13: Favoritism

This is a very touchy subject regarding how two sisters can become so close that the main reason why they came to answer Jesus's call in the first place was almost completely obliterated! I realized that I was gullible and naive about many topics. However, this was one of those touch and go subjects. No one wanted to admit this kind of activity actually occurred in such a holy place as the convent, cloister, monastery or priesthood.

Sometimes I would notice two sisters acting rather tight together. Where you saw one sister you would *sure as shootin* see the other one tagging close behind. I witnessed these things happening all too often. Would all these raunchy, racy little cliques prompt this fledgling sister to think that perhaps it may be time to imitate the career of that great detective Sherlock Holmes? If this sort of debauchery existed in the smaller missionary homes, then what in the world was going on behind closed doors in the Mother House?

February 1994
Krysten & Michaella

This leaves such a sour taste in the pit of my stomach, that I am even ashamed to utter it here in this book. Does this kind of behavior smack of Lesbianism to you?

Today this subject grips the nation. Homosexuality is not only rampant in our country but has its frozen fingers intertwined around each country and continent of this entire planet. It has not only worked its way insidiously throughout our social and cultural networks, but it has infected our family units. Where is the devil amidst all of this turmoil and trouble? He is laughing mightily about all of the chaos he and his cohorts are causing around the globe. I am sure that many of my readers are reeling from a state of shock....then again....maybe not! The only proof that may give credence to my words would be to to tell you that I had been propositioned myself. My body was gripped with fear and trepidation!

Meredith, Jenna, and Matthew
Christmas 1993

Now I must push onward toward the prize who is waiting for me at the end of the finish line - Jesus, who is my peace, joy and hope.

I do not wish to portray most of my convent life as being full of bumps, bruises, weeds and thorns because that is not entirely true. There were times of unspeakable joy and bliss. This is only just a single instance. But whenever I needed a pick-me-up, Jesus was always close at Hand.

I vividly recollect the following incident. Several Sisters of Charity just happened to be in the Mother house Chapel for the culmination of the beautiful Easter season. The Body of the Crucified Christ Who hung upon the Cross during the whole forty days of Lent was now being gently taken down from the Gibbet of the Cross only to be replaced by the Glorified Christ. I was already perched atop the ladder, ready to receive the Alleluia Jesus! Would Our Lord want to extend a small favor to me in exchange for my service to Him? The Messiah's time does not exactly fit into ours. It was not until Morning Mass when I was kneeling at the Communion railing ready to receive the Risen Christ that I received double portion of Holy Communion! Thank You, Sweet Jesus. I love You!

Michaella
February 1994

I want to conclude my convent capers by recalling several incidents involving the Mother Foundress (Mother Snapper) of this recently formed order of sisters and the Mother General (Mother Barker), the president. The final conclusion of my book will sum up what happened after my departure from the religious life, which could be the basis for another book that would describe my life after leaping out of those convent enclosures. Now let us settle in for the *rest of the story.*

Fred & Michaella - Dec. 1994

Chapter 14: Red Hot Rebuttal

One convent caper that stays embedded in my brain like peanut butter on toast was a confrontation that took place between Mother Marie Snapper and approximately twenty young sisters who were seated in the conference room waiting for instructions concerning the examination of conscience as reviewed by Mother Snapper. Guess what? Who do you think would be singled out to be slammed down on the red carpet AGAIN? If you guessed me, you guessed Right!

Matthew,Krysten, Meredith, Jenna, and Michaella - December 1993

I really think that one of Mother Barker's sickest pet peeves was to see how many times she could humiliate me in front of large groups of other sisters. Why was I always used as the scape goat? After all, I was not some kind of rabble-rousing trouble maker! She would even abase me over something as insignificant as my eyeglasses! What was so harmful about those? I failed to see the point.

There were so many times this sly snake would recoil to sink her forked teeth to strike that everyone tried running Helter Skelter. Each time, left alone in the center of the red-ringed bull's eye, trembling, scared, and on the verge of a panic attack, was me. Oh well, Jesus knew all along that I offered myself as a *victim soul* to my Heavenly King for the salvation of souls.

There are so many other convent capers I can recall. I could literally go on and on *ad infinitum,* but that cannot be in my case. Let us now hasten to end. Let's skip down that *yellow brick road* and discover the end of the story.

December 1994 - New Bikes!

Chapter 15: Final Kick in the Pants

I now had some major soul searching to do as to what this poor, bedraggled, defenseless sister was to do. At the tender age of twenty-nine, when I discovered I had to have a 5th knee operation - this time on my right knee - I knew I could NOT teach my students from a wheelchair. There was only one option available. I made an appointment to see Mother Barker to discuss - face to face - my seemingly bleak future.

Mom & me in Piqua - Christmas 1994

That day will be etched in my memory until the end of time – Friday, May, 16, 1980. The bark of the Mother General was louder than her bite as she scowled while calling my name, “Come in, Sr. Josepha and have a seat.” I sheepishly sat down and waited for the face-off. “Let's get straight to point!” Mother Barker taunted, and Round One was off to a frenzied start. “The point is, (I squeaked) I have been mentally, physically and spiritually defeated.” There was a moment of dead silence. In fact, that's the LONGEST New York minute I ever spent in my life. Now both sets of eyes were locked in confrontation. This was going to be a short fight to the finish.

I immediately settled into the tall, hard-backed chair. I searched deep within my soul and found one final hurrah left in me. With a sharp blow to Mother Barker's persona, I countered that I had given the very best years of my life doing SLAVE LABOR for these unrelenting, old sisters. I worked clearing and leveling the land with other sisters in preparation for a new girl's high school gymnasium.

After a few days of grueling labor like that, we limped away with more bumps, bruises, cuts and POISON IVY than I dare speak about. Taking a low blow to Mother Barker's gut, I asked had the Mother ever thought about all the money saved by us being pressed into service for such a monumental task? What a cast of penny pinching tight-wads!

Big snow in Piqua
January 1994

As I set in for the final kill, this wily fox did a big turnaround on me. I felt deep in my heart that drastic changes had to be made. Mother Barker bellowed right into my ear: "Well, you might as well leave right now."

That sent a spinal shock shivering down my back. I took a final gasp as Sister Mary Josepha. Glaring back at Her Reverence, I stood my ground and and bleated like a mild-mannered lamb, "I thought you would have the decency to allow me to graduate my 8th Grade class ." "You couldn't do it anyway," she shot back like a hot arrow. I did not really want to believe what I was hearing!

Jenna
February 1994

After a deathly moment of silence, I submissively asked, "If it would not be too demanding on your schedule, would you give me a ride to the AAA office so I can purchase a plane ticket home?" Mother Barker defiantly demanded, "You just better be out of here by tomorrow." I scolded, "Come on, Mother Barker, I don't know if I can get a plane ticket home that soon. After all, my mother's home is in Charleston, South Carolina, and this is Baltic, Connecticut!" She responded, "Well, then, you be out by Sunday." And with that said, she shoved some money in an envelope and thrust it to me.

That, my dear readers, is the end of the story. Really? Absolutely not! I was actually put out like a thief in the cold, bitter night - secretly, in silence, and ALONE!

Me & the Kids
February 1994

Epilogue

It may seem like a monumental task to try tie up all loose ends, but with God, all things are possible. Someone once gave this advice, "When God closes a door somewhere, He opens a window somewhere else." Then with eyes lifted up to Heaven and and arms out stretched to my Loving Spouse, "Do you mean that ALL this time I was doing my own will?"

Jenna & Michaella in the snow - February 1995

Look how patient and gentle Jesus has been with me. Now, however, my story takes a drastic turn. In a brief time span, Jesus finds the perfect match made from Heaven for me. He gifted Fred to me along with four beautiful daughters and one handsome son.

I was also entrusted with another package at my door. This is the cross of Cancer and could be the source of another new book with the title ***I Surrender ALL***. I simply must wait upon the will of the Lord to see what He chooses to give me. I would like to shout out a special ***God Bless You*** to all who have read this book.

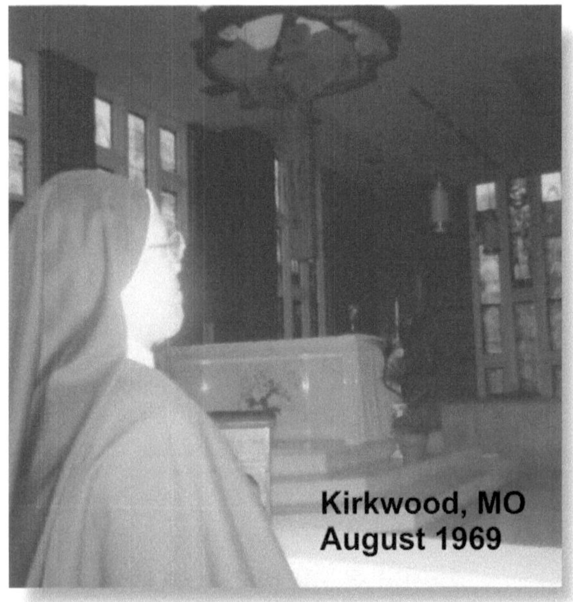

More Photos

Things are really not as "cool, calm and collected as they may seem During the recitation of vows sheepish Fred bleated out, "Take this sign as a ring of my love", while I muttered under my breath, "I can't believe he just said that!" Thankfully the second time round worked like a charm. We were married on August 1, 1981.

Our regular Plant Shutdown - July of 1993. We visited my mother at her Johns Island, SC home. This picture was taken in the Florida room. People from back to front - My mom - Omah (never ask a woman her age!!) holding Michaella - 4 months, to my mom's right is Meredith - 12 years, to Meredith's right is Krysten - 14, in front of the two girls is Matthew – 10, and in front of Matthew is Jenna – 8.

This was taken at our present home on 821 Broadway St., Ohio in 1994. From left to right: Matthew – 9, Jenna – 3, Valli – 41, Meredith – 12, and Krysten – 13.

December 25, 1999. Here is our family at Glenn's house in Raleigh, NC. We had driven down to see Glenn and watch the acorn drop at the New Years Eve festival called First Night Raleigh. It was a cool experience. Ages of our 5 children: Krysten – 16, Meredith – 15, Matthew – 13, Jenna – 8, and Michaella – 6.

This photo was taken in 1951. From left to right is Valli, Christine (my mother's mother), Louise (my mother), and Glenn (my brother). We flew up to Elizabeth, New Jersey to spend some time with Christine at her beautiful Jefferson Avenue home.

1960. Jefferson Avenue after a snow. Steve and Christine sold this home and moved to Bradley Beach in 1961. This lovely home was later torn down to make way for cheap townhouses. What a waste.

Photo taken in Tampa, Florida in 1951. From left to right: Valli, Louise, Glenn, and James.

Christmas – 1952. Valli, Louise, and Glenn. This picture may have been taken in Iselin, NJ where we lived for a brief time. Iselin is only ten miles or so from Elizabeth.

Birthday party in 1952. Photo was probably taken in Iselin, NJ. I can't remember if the party was mine or Glenn's. My father was working as a machine operator at a plant. He was laid off on October 29, 1952. He later went to live with his parents in Clearwater, FL, while Louise, Glenn, and I moved in with my grandmother in Elizabeth, NJ.

Glenn and me. Christmas 1952. Photo was probably taken at my grandmother's house in Elizabeth.

Glenn, mom, and me on Pilot Mountain – December 26, 1953.

Me, Dad, and Glenn on Easter Sunday in 1953. This photo was probably taken in Winston-Salem, NC. Dad moved us there after he got a job at the Big Bear grocery store.

Me, my mom, and Glenn at his birthday party on June 8, 1953. This photo was taken in my grandmother's back yard in Elizabeth, NJ. We must have gone up for a visit.

Glenn on his little, red tractor and me. This was taken in the driveway of my grandmother's house. A little while later, Glenn was peddling down the drive, turned too sharply, and fell off his tractor. He was skinned up pretty bad. Some of Steve's garages in the background.

Glenn, me, and my big rabbit. This photo was taken at 3623 Cornell Blvd. in Winston-Salem, NC.

Glenn and me on Christmas Day at Cornell Blvd. I got some more dolls for my collection. I'll never forget the angel hair we used to put on our trees.

We're having a party on the 4th of July at my grandmother's home. From left to right: Dad, Glenn, Mom, Steve (Pop Pop) and me. I believe the white dog (Husky) at the lower left is Steve's. Copper, mom's Cocker Spaniel is partially in the picture at the bottom. You can see more of Steve's outbuildings on the right. He kept birds of many varieties. They also grew fruit trees and berry yielding bushes. My grandmother was famous for her currant jam.

Me, Mom, Glenn, and Copper on December 27, 1956 at our Cornell Blvd. home. We moved to Charlotte, NC sometime after school was out in 1957.

Glenn and me having a grand old time in Mt. Pleasant, NJ in June 1956. Check out that huge carousel in the background.

We had some friend's, the Brantley's, who owned a farm in NC. This photo was taken during one of our visits. Dad, Mom, Glenn, and me in front of the barn. One thing I remember was the severe cut Mom got on her leg when she tried to climb over a fence topped with barbed wire. That was a nasty wound.

Christmas photo in our home at 3625 Tuckaseegee Road, Charlotte, NC.

630 Jefferson Ave, Elizabeth, NJ, in July 1957. What a magnificent home. There were so many places to explore.

Copper and Chess, my grandmother's beautiful collie, in the back yard of Jefferson Ave.

Me, Glenn, and Mom at Myrtle Beach, SC, in August 1957. I'm sure Dad took the photo. Mom was smoking back then. She quit cold turkey in 1965 and never took up the habit again.

I'm swimming in the canal at Shore Acres, NJ, in July 1957. Uncle Ogden and Aunt Bea owned a vacation there.

A family photo taken at Christmas, 1958. We are now living at 1141 Pauline Ave., Charleston, SC. Dad moved us to McCalls Corner on June 1, 1958. From left to right: Maurice (my Dad's father), Glenn, Louise, Dad, me,and Edith (my Dad's mother). Dad is petting Copper.

Christmas dinner – 1959. Mom, Glenn, and me. Dad took the photo.

March 3, 1959. My birthday party. Glenn is standing in the doorway behind the cake. This photo was taken at our McCalls Corner home. We moved to 468 Trapier Dr. in April. Trapier Dr. was the first home my Dad purchased new. All our other homes were rentals.

My Mom and her two dogs, Alex (left) and Kiwi (right), at Christmas on Johns Island, SC in 1995. Mom passed four years later.

Mom with her Christmas present.
December 25, 1994

Addendum

Bat Exchange

The day of my temporary profession loomed upon me like the plush green valley mixed with all kinds of variegated plants and flowers. You know who was the proudest petunia of the whole bunch? None other than my very own mother. She was all decked out like she was going to the opera followed by a huge regalia after a feast!!! This was so unlike her looking on at my entrance into the Novitiate at the Carmelite Monastery in Jefferson City, MO., where we went to see her in the parlor behind the steel grate. I recall with a vivid memory how she shook those bars and cried out with the voice of an angry bull, "When are you going to come to your senses and get out of that place"? It was just like the devil when he tempted Jesus after He fasted after having gone forty days without food. "Throw yourself down from this pinnacle, worship me and I will give you riches untold of." Jesus rebuked the devil and calmly

Michaella's Birthday Party
March 8, 1995

stated, "Man does not live on bread alone but by every word that comes from the Mouth of God!" With that the devil left Jesus like a drowned rat with his tail between his legs.

I remember that it was a hot, sultry day with high humidity in the air! This Mother House was quite old, and at that time in 1975, central air conditioning would have cost a small fortune, particularly in a mansion that was built before the 1900's!!!

One of our older sisters had an ingenious idea, but this was not well-liked among most of our other sisters. First of all, in order to get to the Chapel, we had to creep past the auditorium. There would go Sr. Gerard Magellan opening up all the windows on her nightly jaunt. There was just one major flaw which all of the sisters were keenly aware of. This story actually stated the true age of this building. The windows that were being opened had NO screens so any kind of creepy, crawling flying bird could come roaring through just like a most unwelcome guest!

I recall that after all the festivities were winding down, we went to the Chapel for the recitation of Compline or Evening Prayer. Much to our chagrin, Sr. Michelle and myself served as lectors. As soon as we stood up we noticed a black dive bomber coming in at 90 degrees sharp. I pretended I was like a Slinky and dove into the safety of the wooden bench, my safe haven. We outsmarted that ole dingbat!!!!

Krysten - March 12, 1995

I still had one more job to do before retiring for the night. I had the job of being sacristan where I would set things out for Mass the next morning. Apparently our fiendish friend had been waiting in the dark sacristy for this unsuspecting sister to fall headlong into this bat exchange. Well, I hurriedly filled the cruets - one with water and one with wine, put the candles on the altar and hightailed it out of the Chapel. I had to make one last stop before heading to my Cell (sounds like a prison) and that would take me down two flights of stairs to the Novitiate. How does that old saying go, "Hindsight is 20/20."

For sure I thought I was in the clear now!!! All I had to do was to put both feet on solid ground and I would be free and clear of that dim witted bird for good!!!! Oops, my bad!!! Just because I made a slip of the tongue and said the bat was bird instead of a mammal, this bat was out to get me but good!!!

As soon as I put my left foot so quietly on the floor, the coast was perfectly clear. Then when my right foot hit the floor, the next thing I knew I was being chased by this ugly, gray bat. It screeched suddenly to a blind halt just 1/8 of an inch from my nose. As I screamed, the bat made a 360 degree turn and headed for the conference room. I made a mad dash to the lavatory. The next minute I knew here comes Sister Teresa Marie running toward the Novitiate armed with a broom, mop, bucket and a sheet to do battle with the bat. This quick skirmish ended quite suddenly and the bat came away with the short end of the stick. The sisters came away victorious this time!!!!

The Catholic Digest

Now that I've taken you through a journey through several states during the years I caught the irresistible convent urge, a question will probably arise - a perfectly legitimate one. Stick around a little bit longer to see how a sister with temporary vows left the convent and within the space of fifteen months had the courage to throw down the gauntlet and challenge the devil to a REAL fight. The quest would be this: How would I, now at the age of twenty-nine years of age, give up, until now, the only life I knew - my Sweet Carmel (which lasted a bit over two years) and being a Sister of Charity at the Mother House and surrounding satellite houses in Taftsville, Willimantic and Manchester (which lasted another ten years). How could I possibly get a dispensation from Our Holy Bishop of Rome to free me from my duties of my vows and get married all before I reached thirty-two?

As I stated before, I knew that when I taught school as a Sister of Charity the habit commanded a sense of respect from all the students. Without it, when I would be in lay person's clothing, how would that effect my presence when I taught in a Catholic or a public school setting? Jesus, You have always shown me the way before. Now I must lean on you even harder!

Here is a gigantic leap of faith that I had to take. Remember when Jacob, who was one of Jesus' bright shining arrows, felt, I should say, KNEW, that with the Lord God with him in battle, Jacob knew in his brain that victory would inevitably be his. However, the dumb devil thought he had outsmarted the TOP GENERAL himself. No way, Jose! Yet, Jacob emerged from battle a little lame in his hip.

So here I am, all ready to board the plane which would be winging me homeward to James Island. My mom would be waiting with bells on! As for me, the last instruction I would receive from Mother Barker was this, "There is one more avenue you may want to consider: Welfare!" Now with that water under the bridge, so to speak, my mom and I embraced each other warmly. I knew that come tomorrow I would be knocking at the College of Charleston's doors. Time to consider a career change. Needless to say, I did much research into what niche I would fit. You may be surprised at what I was really looking into. M-E-N - the marrying kind. My biological clock was like a ticking time bomb ready to explode in a single second. Being a staunch Catholic, when I left the convent I shook the dust from my sandals and vowed that I would forever belong to Jesus alone. Clothes, after all, do NOT make the person; it is what dwells in the heart that God the Father, Jesus, the Son and God, the Holy Spirit, will scrutinize. Do not forget ONE great important truth, the Holy Trinity is ALL MERCIFUL! No matter what you have done, if you demonstrate true remorse for your sin, even though your garment be crimson red, when you wash your garment in the BLOOD of the LAMB, it will become as white as the freshly falling snow! FORGIVEN & FORGOTTEN!

Jenna's first communion.
Easter - March 1997

Now I would begin my prayer in earnest. Jesus, find a good man who is not a smoker, not a drinker and follows the words that God the Father has uttered. After I enrolled in a few courses at college, I stopped at the drugstore's magazine rack. What did I see right at my fingertips - the Catholic Digest! In it lay a goldmine of information. Naturally, I paid for the men's list. I wanted a man who loves Jesus with his whole heart. As I perused the men who made the cut, one gentleman stood out headlong above the rest. I could not understand what kind of nut would write this in his profile: "...am looking for EX-Nuns or postulants." I thought this prince had fallen headlong off his saddle! That was the first big RED strike against him. Then I saw his name - Frederick. I absolutely detested that name! That was the second RED strike against this poor man. The third RED strike - his middle name was Eugene! That was a name I abhorred almost as much as Frederick! Perhaps I should try to meet the computer programmer who lived in New Jersey. Any way, that factory worker would have been thrown out at first base. He didn't know the least bit about playing sports!

Valli - 46th Birthday
March 3, 1997

Somehow, there was something that surrounded this Gentleman #1 with a soft blue shroud that compelled me to write, even though I assumed him to be a creepy guy. I recall that my first letter was written and mailed on January 19, 1981. He opened and read my letter on his birthday - January 22nd. I did discover why he was looking for someone who had been in the religious life. Fred wanted any children we had to be brought up in the Catholic faith. DUH!!! Would you believe he hopped a red-eye flight so we could get to see each other sooner?

I remember Fred telling me he was at St. Mark's Priory, South Union, KY. There was one strange thing about the priests and brothers who resided there. They were allowed to smoke cigarettes and drink beer. Where is the sacrifice in these vices? All I know is that God's timing is perfect, and if this dude was blowing smoke I would say Sayonara to ole Freddie boy. Were wedding bells ringing? You got it! Fred and I were married on August 1, 1981. We spent our honeymoon at Pigeon Forge, TN. After our week long frolic in the summer sun, we were now settling down to family matters.

www.ingramcontent.com/pod-product-compliance
Ingram Content Group UK Ltd.
Pitfield, Milton Keynes, MK11 3LW, UK
UKHW041938190726
13854UKWH00004B/1671

9 781329 129917